WHIPLASH!

Other Books by James L. Percelay

Snaps

Double Snaps

Triple Snaps

Snaps 4

WHIPLASH!

America's Most Frivolous Lawsuits

JAMES L. PERCELAY

WITH JEREMY DEUTCHMAN,
CONTRIBUTING EDITOR

Andrews McMeel
Publishing
Kansas City

00 01 02 03 04 BAH 10 9 8 7 6 5 4 3 2 1

Library of Congress Cataloging-in-Publication Data

Percelay, James.
    Whiplash! : America's most frivolous lawsuits / James L. Percelay;
contributing editor, Jeremy Deutchman.
        p.   cm.
    ISBN 0-7407-0496-6 (pbk.)
      1. Trials—United States.   2. Frivolous suits (Civil procedure)—United
States.   3. Law—United States—Humor.   I. Deutchman, Jeremy.   II. Title.
KF226.P47   2000
349.73'02'07—dc21   99-40325
                                               CIP

Book designed by R. Scott Rattray of Rattray Design

Dedicated to...

Brilliant Brother Bruce,
Sassy Sabine Percelay,
Merrill, Sheela, David,
and
family and friends.

Also, thanks to Harvard graduate student Jeremy Deutchman,
Andrews McMeel Editor In Chief, Chris Schillig,
and agent Frank Weimann

CONTENTS

DISCLAIMER

AS IS THE CASE with many brilliantly funny comedic works, the humor in this book comes shamelessly at the expense of others. Hard as this may be to believe, the plaintiffs in this book may not share in the amusement of seeing their ridiculous behavior paraded over the pages of what promises to be a best-seller.

In the interest of sparing these humor-impaired individuals and potential litigants any further life embarrassment, we have graciously changed their names. That said, every case discussed in this book is absolutely true and a matter of public record. In fact, most of the suits are so bizarre that I couldn't have made them up if I had tried.

Just in case, the following disclaimers also apply: This book is for external use only; if swallowed, do not induce vomiting; limit one per customer; if swelling, redness, rash, or irritation develops, discontinue use and contact a physician; do not hold this book near an open flame; do not read if seal is broken; wear protective goggles; some assembly required; keep this and all humor books out of reach of children; avoid contact with eyes—if contact occurs, flush immediately with water; must be eighteen to enter; do not read while operating a motor vehicle or heavy equipment; any transmissions or rebroadcasts without the express permission of Major League Baseball are prohibited; explicit lyrics; contents may have settled during shipping; objects in this book may be closer than they appear; allow six to eight weeks for delivery; no user-serviceable parts inside; batteries not included; contains no peanuts; void where prohibited by law; penalties for early withdrawal; abdominal distention may occur; no animals were harmed in the writing of this book.

INTRODUCTION

IT USED TO BE that when someone spilled hot coffee on their lap, they called themselves clumsy. Nowadays, they call themselves a lawyer. Attorneys, those dolled-up devil's advocates, have created the notion that we all can win the legal lottery by suing over situations that could have otherwise been resolved by turning the other cheek—a gesture that now could spark a sexual-harassment suit.

Let's face it, lawyers are the primary culprits for our culture of cashing in. They have turned our courts into comedy clubs with acts like the New York couple who sued for damages after getting hit by a subway train while having sex on the tracks, or the worker who was fired for sexual harassment after discussing with a female coworker the plot of a racy Seinfeld episode.

What does it say about a profession that has spawned so many jokes about its ethics? By the way, what is the difference between a catfish and a lawyer? One is a scum-sucking, bottom-feeding scavenger. The other is a fish. If you think about how much frivolous lawsuits cost us all, it is not funny. On the other hand, you have to laugh at how far these court jesters will go in search of the mother lode.

When it comes to creativity, you just can't top lawyers. After all, they concocted the Twinkies Defense, the Ted Kennedy Defense, the Woody Allen Defense, the Joseph Kennedy Defense, the Menendez Defense, the William Kennedy Smith Defense, the O.J. Defense, the Clinton Defense, and a few thousand others that even the *National Enquirer* did not deem fit to print.

It may be unfair to disparage the entire legal profession for the behavior of only 75 percent of its members, but the fact is many of these legal weasels would (and do) defend pit bulls if they smell a juicy fee at the other end of the leash. In fact, it's probably only a matter of time before one of these bloodsuckers sues me for writing this book. But I'll just plead temporary insanity!

Whiplash! America's Most Frivolous Lawsuits is the first compilation of America's most capricious cases and definitively answers the question "Why does everyone hate lawyers?"

LAWSUITS
MADE EASY

WITH TONY BUTTAFONY . . .

Accidents can happen, especially with proper planning!
Just follow Tony's tips for slipping onto *easy street* . . .

Move #32   Move #32A

The Supermarket Slip. You just can't beat this classic move. Simply drop a grape onto your supermarket floor and step on the slippery pulp. Take a bad fall and hire a good lawyer—you'll soon be in the produce business!

The Third Degree. Hot coffee spills are an exciting new area of accident litigation. To cash in on this hot trend, just slice the bottom of your coffee cup, ask for a refill, and get ready for a scalding cup o' lawsuit. This legal maneuver can turn a Starbucks into megabucks—for you!

Move #62A

Move #62

The Chop Suey. Ahhh . . . the elegant chopstick. So simple, yet so deliciously dangerous. When most people see chopsticks they think dumplings, but when lawyers see chopsticks they think opportunity. These unwieldy wooden stakes can splinter, make food drop on your lap, or even poke an eye out. So the next time you eat Chinese, think about ordering *lawsuit-to-go*—it might be your opportunity for good fortune.

Move #21

DRESS FOR COURTROOM SUCCESS

WITH TONY BUTTAFONY...

How you dress says a lot about you—especially before a gullible jury. Mix 'n'match these fashionable courtroom accessories to create that special look that screams, "pain and suffering."

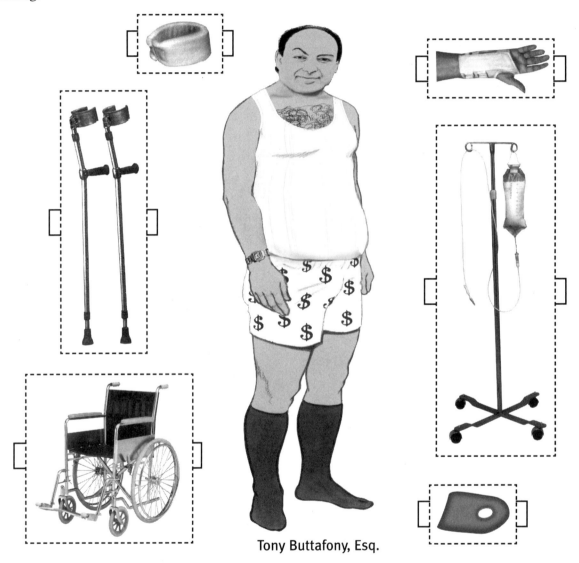

Tony Buttafony, Esq.

THE
WHIPLASH!
AWARDS

for . . .

Outstanding achievement in creating the most
baseless, groundless, and frivolous lawsuits.

Judged by a panel of distinguished
ambulance chasers from around the country.

Congratulations to the winners!

AMERICA'S MOST FRIVOLOUS LAWSUITS...

FALSE
ADVERTISING

The Case of . . .

"FOR WHOM THE BELLE DIDN'T TOLL"

Richard I. Wycoff, Plaintiff, v.
Emporium Videos, Defendant,
in the Supreme Court of Wyoming

An excited Richard Wycoff inserted his newly acquired porn video, *Belle of the Ball,* into his VCR. The movie starred the voluptuous Busty Belle, an "actress" whose talents Mr. Wycoff long admired. However, after watching the tape, Wycoff's enthusiasm went limp. During this seventy-five-minute-long production, Ms. Belle graced the screen for less than ten minutes!

Richard Wycoff (heretofore referred to as "Dick") gave the film "two thumbs down" by suing Emporium Videos, where he bought the video, alleging deceptive trade practices and misrepresentation. Dick sought reimbursement for the cost of the video, cost of medication to treat an asthma attack "brought on by the stress and strain of being ripped off," and additional compensation, presumably for emotional stress caused by his disappointment and frustration.

The Verdict, Please . . .

Reaching a decision on this case was not hard. The judge came to the conclusion that Wycoff's case would not stand up in court and dismissed it. Hopefully, the plaintiff at least rewound his tape before returning it.

The Case of . . .
"LAWSUIT LIGHT"

Richard Underwood, Plaintiff, v. Anheuser-Busch Company, Defendant,
in the Court of Appeals of Michigan

No matter how many times Richard Underwood popped open a Bud Light, the babes in the Budweiser commercials never materialized. Underwood eventually became hopping mad and sued brewmeister Anheuser-Busch for not delivering the fantasy life implied in their ads. He claimed that their curvaceous commercials distracted him, along with the general public, from the health risks associated with excessive drinking. This caused him "physical and mental injury, emotional distress, and financial loss." The perturbed plaintiff went to court to nip this case of false advertising in the bud.

The Verdict, Please . . .

The judge thought this lawsuit was light and tossed it out. But Underwood's spirits weren't dampened and he delivered his case to the State Supreme Court. Unfortunately, his appeal also fizzled out. Richard, this Bud was not for you.

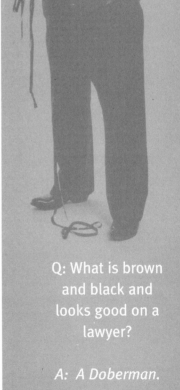

Q: What is brown and black and looks good on a lawyer?

A: A Doberman.

13

The Case of . . .

"THE MISSING MANTRA"

*Robert Nevens, Plaintiff, v. Maharishi
International University, Defendant,
in the United States District Court, Washington, D.C.*

Robert Nevens was twenty-five when he began his quest for "the perfect state of life" that the Maharishi International University had promised. After spending the next eleven years at the university, it finally dawned on him that his guru's promise of achieving "the perfect state of life" in five years had not materialized.

He was particularly mad that he never learned how to fly, as was also promised by the school. Instead, he had only learned to "hop with his legs folded in the lotus position." Claiming psychological and emotional damage, Nevens testified that his twice-daily practice of chanting a single sound did not reverse the aging process *or* teach him to self-levitate.

The Verdict, Please . . .

After meditating on Nevens's case, the jury took the position that the university had, in fact, misled him. Perhaps on the merits of the case, or maybe for good karma, they awarded him $137,890.

Q: If you see a lawyer on a bicycle, why don't you swerve to hit him?

A: It might be your bicycle.

CASES OF COJONES

The Case of . . .
"THE SAW LOOSER"

Thomas Offitz, Plaintiff, v. Dr. Tad E. Grenga, Defendant, in the Norfolk City Circuit Court, Norfolk, Virginia

Thomas Offitz was using a circular saw at a construction site when he noticed a strange branding on his right hand. He was certain that the "666" he saw was the mark of the devil. Recalling the Biblical admonition "If thy hand offend thee, cut it off," Offitz felt that he had no choice: The hand would have to go. Wielding the saw, Offitz sliced off the offending appendage at the wrist. His aghast coworkers immediately scooped up the hand, packed it in ice, and had Offitz and his body part airlifted to nearby Sentara Norfolk General Hospital.

Doctors convinced Offitz to allow them to reattach his hand, but before surgery he changed his mind. Fearing the hand would let Satan take a hold of him, he preferred to live with a handless stump rather than possess the devil's hand. Given Offitz's demands, the surgeons were forced to close the stump.

Less one hand and several months later, Offitz suddenly came to his senses. He missed his hand, and blamed Dr. Tad Grenga for listening to his instructions not to reattach it. He sued the doctor for a handsome $144,000.

The Verdict, Please . . .

It was clear to the jury that Offitz had lost his grip on reality. They single-handedly agreed to throw out his lawsuit. Given the facts of the case, the jury felt that Offitz could only point the finger of blame at himself.

Q: How many lawyers does it take to roof a house?

A: *Depends on how thin you slice them.*

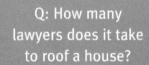

The Case of . . .
"BLIND JUSTICE"

Susan Faith and Reverend Ian Faith, Plaintiffs, v. Southeastern Guide Dogs, Inc., Defendant, in the Manatee Circuit Court

An impoverished blind man named Vernon Henley was thrilled when he received the gift of a seeing-eye dog. The two took their maiden voyage to a shopping mall, where they came upon Susan Faith. The woman saw them coming, but did not move out of their way because she "wanted to see if the dog would walk around me." The dog tugged at his leash, but Henley didn't change directions fast enough, accidentally stepping on Faith's toe and breaking it. Faith could not believe the gall of the blind man.

After learning that Henley had no money, Faith sued the dog's owner, Southeastern Guide Dogs, for "loss of earning capacity . . . and mental pain and suffering." Her husband, Reverend Ian Faith (yes, Reverend), felt he also deserved compensation for the loss of his wife's care, comfort, and consortium. The Faiths refused Southeastern's offer to cover $5,000 worth of medical bills. Vernon Henley died, but the couple kept the faith and soldiered on with their case.

The Verdict, Please . . .

After a newspaper article about the lack of faith shown by the plaintiffs, the couple was inundated with furious phone calls. Reverend and Ms. Faith then decided to be good Christians and they turned the other cheek. After dropping their claim, their born-again law firm, Mulock, Thompson, and Little, followed suit and donated $1,000 to Southeastern Guide Dogs.

Q: What do you call one hundred skydiving lawyers?

A: Skeet.

The Case of . . .

"THE BURNING LOINS"

William Burns, Plaintiff, v. California Savings and Loan and the City of Oakland, Defendants, in the Alameda County Superior Court

William Burns wanted to rob his bank in peace and quiet. But a quick-thinking teller put an end to that when she slipped a tiny smoke bomb into the bag of cash he demanded. As Burns was making his exit from the bank, smoke billowed from the bomb that he had unknowingly placed in his pocket.

The thief now had a problem bigger than his impending arrest. The bomb was getting *real hot* and Burns suffered second- and third-degree burns around his genitals. The device was so hot, in fact, that when the police finally caught up with him, he was "clutching his groin and saying 'ow, ow,' or words to that effect."

Burns thought the use of the bomb was barbaric, and while serving his eight-year term for the robbery, decided to fight back. He sued both California Savings and Loan and the City of Oakland, claiming that the bank's bomb was "inherently dangerous" and the police embarrassed him by "making derogatory and insulting comments about his homosexuality . . . and about his serious injuries."

The Verdict, Please . . .

When the smoke cleared, Burns moved for summary judgment (an immediate ruling in his favor), but the court threw cold water on that motion. His case in ashes, the plaintiff dismissed the suit. The question remains, "Was that a smoke bomb in his pocket, or was he just happy to see the teller?"

18

The Case of . . .
"DON'T SHOOT SO HARD"

Edward Ranset, Plaintiff, v. Linford Richardson,
Terry Frizell, Ronald O. Loveridge,
and Jack Smith, Defendants,
in the United States Court of Appeals
for the Ninth Circuit

Edward Ranset broke into a house, tied up the occupants, shot two of the people (one of them point-blank in the neck), and then fled the scene. One of the victims managed to untie himself and call the police. Officers responded quickly and chased Ranset on foot. When he ignored their orders to stop, Ranset was shot by the cops. He pled guilty to numerous felony counts (it turns out he had permanently blinded one of the men he had shot) but wondered why the police had to be so rough. This incredulous criminal sued the chief of police and three others, accusing them of excessive force.

The Verdict, Please . . .

Perhaps demonstrating the need for higher juror standards, a Riverside jury found in favor of the plaintiff and awarded Ranset $184,000. However, a trial-court judge shot down their dubious decision. A court of appeals also agreed to muzzle the plaintiff's claim.

Q: What do you call a lawyer who doesn't chase ambulances?

A: Crippled.

19

The Case of . . .

"FAIR IS FARE"

Carlos T. Figuerido, Plaintiff, v. Luxor Cab Company, et al., Defendants, in the San Francisco County Superior Court

Carlos Figuerido threw down a tourist, grabbed her purse, and fled. He just might have gotten away with his cowardly crime had it not been for cabbie Holden Hollom. Shouting to his passenger that his ride was now free, Hollom stepped on the gas and chased the crook, until pinning him against a building with his cab. Figuerido gave up and Hollom made a citizen's arrest. The city lauded the courageous cabbie, but Figuerido was not so appreciative—it turns out that his leg was broken as a result of what he alleged to be "excessive force and negligence in effecting the citizen's arrest." Figuerido, who was later convicted, sued Hollom and his cab company.

The Verdict, Please . . .

A California jury took the heroic Hollom for a ride by assessing him $24,595 for the injuries suffered by the purse snatcher. But justice was finally metered out when the verdict was overturned. Figuerido's lawyer, defending himself over the public outcry resulting from the case, pleaded: "I'm just a lawyer."

Q: Why did the post office recall the new lawyer stamps?

A: Because people could not tell which side to spit on.

20

The Case of . . .
"WRONG-WAY JUSTICE"

Matthew T. Andrews, Plaintiff, v. The Estate of Sigmund and Irene Fitz, Defendant,
in the Oakland County Circuit Court

Matthew Andrews was driving down the wrong side of the highway when he plowed into Sigmund and Irene Fitz's car, killing them both. Because police failed to follow proper procedures in Andrews's blood-alcohol test, it was ruled inadmissible, and the drunk driver only had to plead guilty to a charge of negligent homicide, pay a $400 fine, and serve two years' probation.

Five years later, Matthew Andrews was a depressed man and felt that the late Fitzes were to blame. He now wanted money and sued the Fitz estate, asserting that he often felt he would be "better off dead." Andrews himself suffered injuries from the accident, but his nerve was obviously intact as evidenced by his assertion that the Fitzes "had the time, the opportunity, and the ability to avoid this accident" by swerving into another lane.

The Verdict, Please . . .

Andrews crossed the line on this suit by blaming his dead victims for his living hell. It didn't take long for the jury to total his case and find for the defendant.

Q: Why should lawyers wear lots of sunscreen when vacationing at a beach resort?

A: *Because they're used to doing all of their lying indoors.*

SUITS
FROM THE
SLAMMER

The Case of . . .
"NO-PENIS ENVY"

*Thomas I. Greene, Plaintiff, v. Harold Farrier and
Crispus C. Nix, Defendants,*
in the United States Court of Appeals
for the Eighth Circuit

Thomas Greene was tired of being "cruelly imprisoned in a man's body," so he sued the State of Iowa for a sex-change operation. Thomas, who prefers to go by "Tammy," was serving a ten-year sentence for armed robbery. He began his sex-change campaign with letters to the prison warden pleading that he "could not stand the emotional stress. The penis has to go now."

The warden denied Greene's request, writing back that "some of the [prison] staff are baffled as to why you want perfume, cosmetics, and women's clothing when you are wearing a mustache. A mustache does not accent your femininity." Undeterred, Greene sued for his "right" to electrolysis, cosmetic surgery, hormone therapy, a sex-change operation, female clothes and cosmetics, and a transfer to a women's prison.

The Verdict, Please . . .

The *penal* system sounds like the perfect place for this plaintiff. Unfortunately, his ruling turned out to be a drag. An appeals court judge agreed with the warden that "the State has a legitimate interest in not having a male with female breasts in a male prison," though perhaps Greene's fellow prisoners may have disagreed.

Q: How can you tell
there's an afterlife for
lawyers?

A: *Because after they
die, they lie still.*

23

The Case of . . .

"PRISONER OF LOVE"

Derek B. Ratan, Plaintiff, v. Phyllis B. Woods, Defendant, in the United States Court of Appeals for the Fourth Circuit

Behind bars for first-degree rape, Derek Ratan got his kicks out of filing meritless lawsuits against female judges, lawyers, and correctional officials. In one claim he alleged that a female judge had a crush on him. In another, he sued Warden Phyllis Woods, claiming that the pair had an affair and that Woods offered him money to assassinate her husband.

The plaintiff's claim was not measuring up as he proceeded to allege that when the couple had sex Woods would cry out, "Please don't, you're tearing me open." According to Ratan, Woods then confessed to him her real problem: "that she could not take all nine inches."

The Verdict, Please . . .

The court castrated the plaintiff's case and cut short his campaign of sexual harassment. He was barred from making future claims without the permission of a judge and fined for abusing the legal system. The only thing not guilty about this sleazy character was his conscience.

Q: What can a goose do, a duck can't, and a lawyer should?

A: Stick his bill up his ass.

The Case of . . .
"INTEL INSIDE"

Theodore A: Hedron, Plaintiff, v. State of New Jersey, Defendant,
in the United States District Court for the District of New Jersey

While in federal custody, Theodore Hedron made a trip to the Eye, Ear, and Speech Clinic in Newark, New Jersey. After his examination, Hedron claimed the state "unlawfully injected him in the left eye with a radium electric beam." As a result he claimed to hear voices inside his brain—voices that apparently mentioned the number $12 million, the amount for which he sued the State of New Jersey.

The Verdict, Please . . .

Judge Biunno noted "the complaint hinges on a question of presumably unlicensed radio communication, and therefore falls within the purview of the Federal Communications Commission." The jocular judge also pointed out that Hedron could have prevented the broadcast to the "antenna" in his brain simply by grounding it. He went on to explain that the plaintiff would only have had to pin a short chain of paper clips to his pant leg so that they touched the ground, thereby preventing any unwanted conversations inside his brain.

Q: What do you get when you cross the Godfather with a lawyer?

A: An offer you can't understand.

The Case of . . .

"THE PERVERTED PLAINTIFF"

Leonard R. DeSalle, Plaintiff, v. A. J. Arave, Defendant, in the United States Court of Appeals for the Ninth Circuit

Idaho State prisoner Leonard DeSalle could not believe that Warden Arave would not let him receive publications from the North American Man/Boy Love Association (NAMBLA). Claiming the warden didn't understand his needs, the convicted pedophile took his appeal to court. He claimed that the warden's nix on NAMBLA bulletins was not "reasonably related to legitimate penalogical interests." Ironically, it was the plaintiff's same *penal interests* that landed him behind bars in the first place.

The Verdict, Please . . .

The idea of perverting justice did not excite the judge, who denied the pedophile his pamphlets. In fact, the court noted that NAMBLA's newsletters encouraged the same degenerate behavior that had originally put DeSalle behind bars. An appeals court also ruled against this most unappealing character.

Q: What do you buy a friend graduating from law school?

A: A lobotomy.

The Case of . . .
"WHAT'S THE FREQUENCY?"

Lester R. Pincus, Plaintiff, v. Michigan Department of Corrections and Steven A. Myers, M.D., Defendants, in the United States District Court for the Eastern District of Michigan, Northern Division

Lester Pincus resented that his jailers "attempted" and "succeeded" to implant a "telepathic mind-control device" into his brain. He claimed that guards entered his cell, sliced open his head, and slipped in a mind-control microchip. The instrument, he alleged, allowed prison officials to control his every action.

Somehow, managing to act on his own will, Pincus sued thirty-one Department of Corrections employees and a doctor who had assisted in the "cover-up." He sought $1 million in compensatory damages and $10 million in punitive damages from each defendant.

The Verdict, Please . . .

Perhaps the wired Pincus would have been better off in *circuit* court. The judge noted that "as a matter of law, intracranial thought-control devices are far beyond the reach of currently available technology." The judge transmitted his decision to the plaintiff that he was pulling the plug on his frivolous case.

Q: What is the difference between a female lawyer and a catfish?

A: One's slimy and has whiskers, and the other one lives in water.

27

The Case of . . .

"THE DATE FROM HELL"

Anthony C. Anelle, Plaintiff, v. Together of New Hampshire, Defendant, in the Suffolk Superior Court

"A rare find" by his own description, Anthony Anelle was disappointed that the Together of New Hampshire dating service couldn't find him the woman of his dreams. Anelle seemed flexible enough, claiming he would "have no problem swapping a nice body for good looks and vice versa."

But the thirty-two-year-old bachelor was outraged for two reasons. First, because the dates he'd been on were fiascoes (after the first, he called the dating agency and told them, "I asked for the model type, not something from *The Bride of Frankenstein*"), and second, because Together suddenly stopped finding him dates.

When asked why they rejected his business, employees of Together pointed out the obvious: Anelle, also known as inmate "W 44721," was serving a prison term on cocaine charges. The convict protested, "I am at a medium security facility, have contact visits, and will be considered for placement at minimum-prerelease in the months to come." But Together wasn't impressed, so Anelle made a date with them in court.

The Verdict, Please . . .

Together's owner was so mad at having to pay to defend himself against this convicted felon's absurd suit that he didn't appear at the hearing. A superior court judge was forced to find him in default for standing up the claimant in court.

Q: Do you know how to save a drowning lawyer?

A: Take your foot off his head.

The Case of . . .
"THE PROLIFIC PLAINTIFF"

*Benjamin Larson, Plaintiff, v. C. Strickland, R.
Dugger, D. Watson, M. Franks, and Two
Unnamed Prison Notaries, Defendants,*
in the United States District Court for the Middle
District of Florida, Jacksonville Division

Within a six-year period, Benjamin Larson filed 176 lawsuits in the
Middle District of Florida alone. In *Larson v. Deering,* the convicted murderer sued a corrections officer who had "denied him
sugar for his coffee and cereal." Then he sued the Florida Department of Corrections for violating his civil rights by "limiting break-
fast to one ounce of juice per day, one roll instead of two, one box
of cereal instead of two . . ." Larson sued again when he got athlete's foot from the prison floor. And no matter how late he stayed
up filing suits, Larson couldn't manage to get himself a decent cup
of coffee: He sued again after being "deprived of thirty spoonfuls
of coffee."

The Verdict, Please . . .

The Sunshine State rained on the plaintiff's parade when it sought
a permanent injunction on his lawsuit-filing ability in Florida. This
not only cast a shadow on Larson's future courtroom activities, but
it was also a dark day for local defense attorneys.

Q: How do you stop a
lawyer from drowning?

A: *Shoot him before he
hits the water.*

The Case of . . .
"A CLOTHES CALL"

Joseph Pelster, Plaintiff, v. Correctional Officer Matthew DeFrank, Defendant,
in the United States District Court for the Southern District of New York

After a corrections officer allegedly stomped on his jacket, convicted felon Joseph Pelster sued Officer Matthew DeFrank for "$989 billion trillion." He also sued the State of New York to erect a luxury building like the Trump Plaza and name it "Pelster Plaza."

The Verdict, Please . . .

Judge Andrew J. Peck sent the case to the cleaners. As for the "$989 billion trillion" and "Pelster Plaza," it seems unlikely that "The Donald" has much to worry about.

Q: If a lawyer and an IRS agent were both drowning, and you could only save one of them, would you go to lunch or read the paper?

The Case of . . .
"ONE HELLUVA LAWSUIT"

Michael P. Sullivan, Plaintiff, v. W. E. Johnson, Defendant,
in the United States Court of Appeals for
the Eleventh Circuit

Prisoner Michael Sullivan just wanted to practice his religion, Satanism. The plaintiff asserted that the warden denied his request for *The Satanic Bible, The Satanic Book of Rituals,* and a Satanic medallion. His religion also demanded wrist slashing, blood drinking, and the consumption of human flesh (usually fingers), and asked its adherents to burn candles made from the fat of unbaptized infants. To alleviate the warden's fears, Sullivan asserted that he genuinely hoped that the person whose flesh is eaten is still alive at the end of the ritual.

The Verdict, Please . . .

The court played devil's advocate and denied Sullivan's request. But perhaps that's all the plaintiff wanted—someone to tell him to "go to hell."

Q: Have you heard about the lawyers' word processor?

A: No matter what font you select, everything comes out in fine print.

The Case of . . .
"THE NON-PROPHET"

Andre Rashad, Plaintiff, v. Garry Henman, Defendant, in the United States District Court for the Southern District of Illinois

Andre Rashad was certain that the feds had the wrong man because *he was actually the Prophet Mohammed.* This resident of the United States Penitentiary in Marion, Illinois, filed a lawsuit against his jailer, Warden Garry Henman. Rashad maintained that he was subject only to Islamic law and as the leader of the Nation of Islam his conviction should be overturned. Rashad had no interest in being a free man if it meant being poor: He also sought unspecified "liabilities" owed to him for his ordeal.

The Verdict, Please . . .

The Prophet Mohammed may have had many followers, but this prison prophet couldn't even follow directions in filing his claim. The judge dismissed the case and was probably pleased that he lost his prophet.

Q: What is the definition of a shame (as in "that's a shame")?

A: When a busload of lawyers goes off a cliff.

Q: What is the definition of a "crying shame"?

A: That there was an empty seat.

The Case of . . .
"THE EXTRA-VIRGIN LAWSUIT"

Samuel A. Sauter, Plaintiff, v. Capital Enterprises, Defendant, in the Pennsylvania Superior Court

Convicted of concocting a bogus 900 number to cheat AT&T out of over $550,000, Samuel Sauter was sentenced to eight years. With all that time on his hands, the amateur chef cooked up another con. His plan was to disprove the Bertolacci olive oil company's claim that its ten-ounce bottles contained 128 tablespoon servings. Using the prison kitchen, he emptied a bottle, tablespoon by tablespoon, until he reached the end. Lo and behold, his test yielded only twenty-one tablespoons—a clear case of fraud!

Sauter sued the olive-oil maker. In so doing he was able to get the court to waive its fees because of his lack of funds—though, over an eighteen-month period, he somehow managed to spend $1,600 at the prison canteen on olive oil to make his signature "all natural" spaghetti sauce.

The Verdict, Please . . .

A panel of judges found Sauter's claim "extremely hard to digest." The plaintiff probably didn't help his case by confiding that, in order to make his gourmet spaghetti sauce, he had to "steal the vegetables from the [prison] kitchen." The judges summarily dismissed the suit and the Bertolacci company had no comment about this slippery character.

Q: What is the difference between God and a lawyer?

A: *God doesn't think he's a lawyer.*

33

The Case of . . .

"HAIR TODAY, GONE TOMORROW"

Samuel Vernon Johnson, Plaintiff, v.
James A. Collins, Defendant,
in the Court of Appeals of Texas,
First District, Houston

The Texas Department of Corrections's hair policy rubbed convicted criminal Samuel Johnson the wrong way. Johnson was perturbed by the prison policy prohibiting any "block, Afro, natural, or shag" haircuts, and decided to put an end to the injustice. The uncoiffed criminal sued, complaining that he had lost his individuality and self-esteem because he wasn't allowed to grow his hair in a way that hid his hair loss.

The Verdict, Please . . .

A Texas trial court felt there wasn't a strand of evidence to legally justify Johnson's claim. The judge cut his case short and dismissed it. The bald truth was that this plaintiff was going to have many bad-hair days ahead of him.

Q: What is the difference between a porcupine and two lawyers in a Porsche?

A: With a porcupine, the pricks are on the outside!

34

The Case of . . .
"NAKED BEFORE GOD"

Richard D. Olsen, Plaintiff, v.
Howard Peters III, et. al., Defendant,
in the United States District Court for the Northern
District of Illinois, Western Division

Federal inmate Richard Olsen claimed to be a devout member of a religious group called "Technicians of the Sacred," a religion that encourages its followers to worship in the nude. Doing time for attempted murder, Olsen complained that he could not get naked in the prison chapel. He sued, alleging that not being able to pray *au naturel* was in violation of his religious freedom.

The Verdict, Please . . .

A judge stripped this case down to its bare essentials and found it frivolous. He dismissed the suit, after which a Corrections Department spokesman commented that it was one of his favorites, along with an earlier one in which an inmate sued after claiming that a bird flew through his cell window and took his peanut butter and jelly sandwich.

Q: How do you know when your divorce is getting ugly?

A: *When your lawyer doesn't seem like a blood-sucking leech anymore.*

PENNSYLVANIA ATTORNEY GENERAL'S TOP 10 FRIVOLOUS INMATE LAWSUITS

10. A prisoner sued fifteen corrections officers claiming, among other things, that his state-issued underwear was too tight, a condition that went uncorrected for fifteen days.

9. A prisoner claimed he was deprived of due process when he was disciplined for having oral sex with a visitor. He claimed his penis "accidentally fell out of his pants."

8. A prisoner alleged that unknown law enforcement officials were sending transmissions to a microchip that Department of Corrections employees had surreptitiously implanted in his brain. These transmissions sometimes interfered with his thinking and caused him pain; at other times, they revealed to him improper motives of others.

7. A prisoner who was a smoker claimed he had the right to be housed in a smoke-free environment.

6. A prisoner who had been suing the state for the last fifteen years claimed that his family owned all the oil and mineral rights in Pennsylvania and Texas and that the governors of those states were trying to murder him in order to deprive him of these rights. Among other things, he wanted $700 million for lost revenues.

5. A prisoner claimed that prison officials violated his First Amendment rights when they refused to let him buy a series of books and magazines featuring themes of rape, bestiality, and incest. Titles included *Gang Bang Family, Cheerleaders Best Orgy,* and *Daughter Love Dog.*

4. Two would-be transsexual prisoners sued to force the taxpayers to pay for sex-change surgery while they were in prison.

3. A prisoner sued over a lack of adequate medical care, claiming that he contracted "cancer incubus" from a cheeseburger, and that a nurse gave him a cup of water laced with "hepatitis incubus."

2. A prisoner claimed that prison officials deprived him of the free exercise of his religion when they refused to allow him to call his Islamic brothers to pray by chanting the call to prayer loudly enough to be heard throughout the cellblock—at 4:00 A.M.

1. A prisoner claimed that he had been denied adequate medical care for a kidney problem and had been disciplined for seeking the care. In fact, he had been seen by medical staff 153 times for baseless complaints. He was disciplined for lying to the staff when he handed a doctor two pea-sized pieces of gravel and claimed they were kidney stones he had just passed.

And, in the "Believe-It-or-Not" category:

Inmate Ronald McDonald sued the Department of Corrections when he was kicked out of a prerelease program and sent back to prison to finish serving his sentence for, what else, stealing hamburgers.

POLLUTED
PLAINTIFFS

The Case of . . .
"THE URINARY TRACK"

Kim Hua Nguyen, Administratrix of the Estate of Bihn Nguyen, Plaintiff, v. Chicago Transit Authority, Defendant, in the Supreme Court of Illinois

Korean immigrant Bihn Nguyen drank heavily at a friend's party. Walking home afterward, he decided to relieve himself by a railway line. Unable to read English, Nguyen passed by signs like DANGER, KEEP OUT, and ELECTRIC CURRENT—not to mention stepping over jagged boards called "jaws," which were intended to prevent pedestrians from trespassing. Nguyen finally stopped near a platform and began urinating onto the tracks. Unfortunately, his stream made contact with the electrified third rail, sending six hundred volts blazing through his body.

Nguyen died quickly and officials found him with his feet pointing toward the third rail, his pants zipper open, and his penis exposed. Soon after the incident, Nguyen's wife, Jae, sued the Chicago Transit Authority, claiming that they should have anticipated the accident and taken further steps to reduce the possibility of electrocution.

The Verdict, Please . . .

An Illinois jury awarded the widow $3 million in damages, which it then reduced by half to acknowledge that Bihn shared some of the responsibility. *Some* of the responsibility, indeed! Bihn's demise was sad, but he sure got quite a *sum* for his share of the responsibility.

Q: What would happen if you locked a cannibal in a room full of lawyers?

A: *It would starve to death.*

38

The Case of . . .
"MY BEER CUP RUNNETH UNDER"

Patrick Jolly and Allen Howe, Plaintiffs, v. Ogden Entertainment Services, Defendant, in the Philadelphia Court of Common Pleas

Patrick Jolly and Allen Howe read a *Philadelphia Daily News* article about the beer at Phillies games possibly being a few sips short per cup. If true, Phillies fans would have been cheated out of an estimated $495,000 in one season alone. The drinking duo filed a class-action suit allowing anyone who purchased a beer between 1994 and 1998 to claim damages for the two ounces of missing beer.

Ogden Entertainment, the vendor, labeled them a couple of "jokers," noting that beer at the game is advertised not by quantity, but by "large" or "small." However, Jolly and Howe insisted that their case was more fact than foam and took their case of beer to court.

The Verdict, Please . . .

The sobering reality was that the plaintiffs' case was flat. Jolly and Howe swallowed their pride and withdrew their claim, but not before getting assurances that Ogden Entertainment would not countersue.

Q: Why do lawyers keep their diplomas on their dashboard?

A: *So they can park in the handicapped spaces.*

39

CELEBRITY
CASES

The Case of . . .

"THE FIRST CUT IS THE DEEPEST"

Susan Peterson, Plaintiff, v. Rod Stewart, Defendant, in the Oakland County Circuit Court

Rod Stewart's concert brought tears to Susan Peterson's eyes. It seems that the rocker kicked a soccer ball into the stadium audience that hit Peterson seated in the twenty-third row. The impact of the ball ruptured her middle-finger tendon and caused "permanent disfigurement."

Claiming that Stewart "is an accomplished soccer kicker" and should have realized that he could hurt someone, Peterson sued the rocker to the tune of $10,000. She further claimed that her injury contributed to the breakup of her marriage since the pain from her finger made sex highly frustrating. Her ex-husband elaborated: "If she hit that hand on something, it was all over."

The Verdict, Please . . .

Rod Stewart testified that since kicking soccer balls into the crowd was a part of his act, he shouldn't be held liable. But his lyrics didn't move the court and he settled to the tune of $17,000. This was not one of Rod's greatest hits.

Q: Did you hear about the new sushi bar catering exclusively to lawyers?

A: It's called "Sosumi."

41

The Case of . . .
"GRAPES OF WRATH"

Omar Rashan, Plaintiff, v. Reverend Robert Schuller, Defendant, in the Brooklyn Federal Court

Reverend Robert Schuller, host of the *Hour of Power* television show, was on a United Airlines flight from Los Angeles to New York. While sitting in first class, he was served fruit and cheese by flight attendant Omar Rashan. He asked Rashan for some extra grapes because of his low-fat diet, but that's where Schuller and Rashan's stories take a different flight path.

According to Schuller, Rashan refused his request for the fruit. At that point the reverend asked another flight attendant for grapes and tried to counsel the angry Rashan by gently placing his hand on Rashan's arm. The flight attendant's story was a bit different. Rashan accused Schuller, a spiritual adviser to presidents from Nixon to Clinton, of screaming, "No! No! I don't want cheese! I can't see cheese! I can't eat cheese! I'm allergic to cheese!" and demanding every grape on board. The twenty-six-year-old Rashan claimed that the seventy-year-old Schuller shook him "so hard my head was going back and forth, giving me whiplash and pain."

Traumatized by the alleged incident, Rashan sued Schuller, claiming that neck and shoulder pain and numbness in his fingers and feet made working impossible.

The Verdict, Please . . .

A fellow first-class passenger verified Schuller's innocence, but Rashan was experienced with turbulence and didn't buckle. Ultimately, Schuller landed a $1,100 fine, had the U.S. Attorney's Office monitor his behavior for six months, and apologized to Rashan for touching him. The reverend maintained his innocence, stating, "I know one thing for sure: God will have the last word, and it will be good."

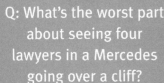

Q: What's the worst part about seeing four lawyers in a Mercedes going over a cliff?

A: A Mercedes seats five.

NUT CASES

The Case of . . .
"SO SUE ME!"

Omir Tobei, Plaintiff, v. Omir Tobei, Defendant, in the Court of Appeals of California, Third Appellate District

Omir Tobei was so upset, he decided to sue . . . himself. Tobei, the plaintiff, claimed that Tobei, the defendant, was beneficiary to a trust fund in his name. The plaintiff was tired of the defendant controlling his estate and tried to revoke his own birth certificate to take control over his money from . . . well, himself. So off Tobei went to court to seek sole possession of his trust.

The Verdict, Please . . .

Judge William Lund didn't think twice about dismissing the claim when Tobei, the defendant, failed to respond to Tobei, the plaintiff's, lawsuit. An appeals court echoed the original decision to dismiss.

Q: What is a criminal lawyer?

A: Redundant.

The Case of . . .
"THE ANNOYED PARANOID"

*Judith Jonas, Plaintiff, v. James Carter, William
Clinton, Ross Perot, American Cyanamid,
Iron Mountain Security Corporation, Defense
Intelligence Agency, IBM, David Rockefeller,
Rockefeller Fund, BCCI, and NASA, Defendants,
in the United States District Court for the
Southern District of New York*

Judith Jonas wanted to blow wide open government "secrets" that
she had recently uncovered. Her lawsuit alleged a conspiracy to
enslave certain groups in our society. Ms. Jonas insisted that as a
cyborg (part human, part computer) she received "inside" telepathic information. She claimed to have uncovered the defendants' plan to reinstitutionalize slavery and alleged that Jimmy
Carter was the secret head of the Ku Klux Klan; that Bill Clinton
is the biological son of Jimmy Carter; and that Clinton and Ross
Perot have made fortunes in the death-hunting industry, and are
responsible for the murder of at least ten million black women in
concentration camps.

The Verdict, Please . . .

This budding conspiracy theorist would have made Oliver Stone
proud, but not so the judge. He noted that "If *this* Court cannot
order dismissal of this complaint . . . no district court can ever
dismiss any complaint."

Q: Why won't sharks
attack lawyers?

A: *Professional courtesy.*

45

The Case of . . .

"SUE YOU, SUE ME"

Lester P. Lucas, Plaintiff, v. Lester P. Lucas, Defendant, in the Norfolk District Court

When Lester Lucas wondered whom he could blame for his twenty-three-year prison sentence, he looked in the mirror and found the culprit. *He* had caused himself to face arrest for grand larceny, and *he* was responsible for his being locked up at the Indian Creek Correctional Center in Chesapeake, Virginia. So who should be forced to pay large sums of cash to him as punishment? Why, *he* should, of course. And who better to represent him in court, but *him*.

The Verdict, Please . . .

It's cases like this that inspired the adage "A person who represents himself has a fool for a client." The plaintiff/defendant/lawyer all went back to his/their cell after the judge rejected his/their case.

Q: What's the difference between a tick and a lawyer?

A: The tick drops off after you're dead.

XXX
FILES

The Case of . . .

"NO THANKS FOR THE MAMMARIES"

Ted Gainer, Plaintiff, v. Tawny Peaks, Defendant, in The People's Court

Beer, boobs, and buddies—what better ingredients for a bachelor party? At least that's what Ted Gainer's friends thought when they took their pal to Diamond Dolls, a renowned strip club in Clearwater, Florida. Headlining that evening was Tawny Peaks, a stripper whose sizable breasts, according to Gainer, packed quite a punch.

During the party, Peaks placed the bachelor in a low chair and told him to lean his neck back so she could "specially entertain" him. She then dropped her breasts down over Gainer's ears, making him, as she put it, "look like Mickey Mouse." But something went horribly awry. According to Gainer's lawyer, Peaks "suddenly, and without warning . . . forced her very large breasts into his face, causing his head to jerk backwards." Gainer further testified that he "saw stars" during her performance and that "Peaks's breasts just about knocked me out . . . It was like two cement blocks hit me."

After enduring two years of pain from whiplash, medical bills, and embarrassment, Gainer decided to take Peaks to *The People's Court* presided over by former New York City mayor Edward I. Koch.

The Verdict, Please . . .

To better weigh both sides of the argument, Mayor Koch sequestered Ms. Peaks in a room with his bailiff Josephine, who put the stripper's breasts on a scale. She found her mammaries to be "about two pounds each and of average firmness." The judge considered these facts and the other mounds of evidence before ruling in favor of Ms. Peaks.

The Case of . . .
"TAKING THE 'F' TRAIN"

Mary Sanchez and Derek Thomas, Plaintiffs, v. New York City Transit Authority, Defendant, in the New York City Transit Authority, Brooklyn

New York City subway conductor Arriaga thought he'd seen it all, until, that is, he spotted a couple making love on the track in front of his speeding train. The stunned driver yanked the emergency brake, but couldn't stop his four-hundred-ton train from rolling over the copulating couple. Rushed to Bellevue Hospital, the victims miraculously survived, though they suffered injuries, including a dislocated pelvis and a broken leg.

Derek Thomas and Mary Sanchez had beaten the odds and then decided to try their luck again by suing the New York City Transit Authority for "carelessness, recklessness, and negligence" in sending a train on a seldom-used track. Derek, by the way, admitted that the night before he had downed "a can of beer" and "maybe heroin, cocaine, I'm not sure."

The Verdict, Please . . .

Six years after hearing their case, the New York City Transit Authority has not heard from the couple nor their attorney—however, the case is still pending. After trying to take the Transit Authority for a ride, it looks like the couple may have left the station.

Q: Why do lawyers wear neckties?

A: To keep the foreskin from crawling up their chins.

XXX

49

The Case of . . .
"THE MIRACULOUS CONVERSION"

Ann Vestry, Plaintiff, v. St. Florian Catholic Church, Defendant, in the Court of Appeals of Wisconsin, District One

Seventy-year-old Ann Vestry was playing bingo over at St. Florian Catholic Church when the electronic scoreboard inexplicably fell off its platform, struck her head, and . . . altered her sexual preference. Vestry asserted in court papers that the blow caused her to become attracted to females, as well as to experience multiple spontaneous orgasms. This was not the kind of epiphany Ann expected to have in church and took her case to an even higher authority—the courts.

The Verdict, Please . . .

Suspecting her case was not in good faith, an appeals judge dismissed Vestry's claim. He noted that by refusing to take a series of psychological tests, she brought the dismissal upon herself. The court also noted that while the plaintiff may have been truly upset by her new sexual orientation, the former heterosexual filed her case some three years *after* the incident.

Q: What do you have when a lawyer is buried up to his neck in sand?

A: Not enough sand.

XXX

The Case of . . .

"ALL MEN ARE DOGS"

Susan Paulson, Plaintiff, v. Howard J. Moraghan, Defendant, in the United States Court of Appeals for the Second Circuit

To examine documents related to pending litigation, Susan Paulson made occasional trips to the courthouse. However, on each visit she felt sexually harassed—not by a court employee, but by a canine. Paulson claimed that "Kodak," Judge Howard Moraghan's dog, would lift her skirt up with his snout and probe around her crotch area while she was researching files. Certain that she saw Moraghan smirking as his dog investigated her, Paulson bit back with a lawsuit. According to her, the judge knew that his pet preferred women in skirts and intended to sexually harass her.

The Verdict, Please . . .

The court ruled that despite her dogged pleas, Ms. Paulson was barking up the wrong tree. The fact that she never claimed to have cut short her visits as a result of her abuse may have helped put her case in the doghouse.

Q: What is the difference between a hooker and a lawyer?

A: A hooker will stop screwing you when you're dead.

51

FOOD
FIGHTS

The Case of . . .

"MILKING THE SYSTEM"

Stanley C. Gordon, Plaintiff, v. Safeway Stores Inc., Defendant,
in Court of the Western District of Washington

"Milk Makes a Body Feel . . . Bad?" That was Stanley Gordon's contention when he suffered a mild stroke. A "lifetime of milk drinking," he claimed, had gotten him addicted to the white stuff which he was certain had done him in. Gordon sued the Washington Dairy Products Commission and Safeway (where he did most of his shopping). Besides money, his suit called for warning labels on dairy products and compensation for the caring of other "milkaholics."

The Verdict, Please . . .

Apparently the judge felt that Gordon's case was utterly ridiculous because he dismissed it. Mr. Gordon didn't get the milk warning labels he sought, but his case did get *The Tonight Show*'s Jay Leno to show a milk-carton label that cautioned: "Too much milk can make you a frivolous lawsuit-filing moron."

THE
WHIPLASH!
AWARD

Q: Where do you find a lawyer who won't screw you?

A: *In the obituaries.*

The Case of . . .
"THE McSHAKES"

William Bailey, Plaintiff, v. McDonald's Corporation, Defendant, in the Supreme Court of New Jersey

John Parker made a pit stop at a McDonald's drive-thru window. After wedging his chocolate milkshake between his legs and putting his burger and fries onto the seat next to him, he headed back onto the road. When Parker leaned over to reach for his fries he inadvertently squeezed his legs together, causing the cold shake to leap out of its cup and onto his lap. A stunned Parker then plowed his car into the vehicle in front of him.

William Bailey, who was at the receiving end of Parker's mishap, was not sympathetic. He sued Parker *and* McDonald's, claiming that the fast-food franchise neglected to warn customers of the dangers of eating and driving.

The Verdict, Please . . .

The judge wasn't stirred, never mind shaken, by Bailey's claim. He dismissed his suit; however, he also denied McDonald's request that Bailey reimburse them for their $10,000 in attorney's fees. In the judges words, Bailey was "creative and imaginative and shouldn't be penalized for that."

Q: How bad was the crash of 1987?

A: It was so bad, the lawyers were walking around with their hands in their own pockets.

54

The Case of . . .
"LAWSUIT PLAIN OR PEANUT"

Edward McBride, Plaintiff, v. M&M/Mars Co., Defendant,
in the Lorain County Common Pleas Court

Edward McBride loved M&M's and had just popped one of the peanut variety into his mouth. Not letting the morsel melt in his mouth, nor in his hands, he chomped down hard. He bit so hard, in fact, that his teeth sailed right through the candy-coated shell, past the creamy milk chocolate center, and into his lower lip.

According to McBride, the M&M in question was missing its peanut and he bit hard anticipating the goober would slow the mashing of his teeth. For his pain and suffering, McBride took a bite out of M&M/Mars, Inc., suing them for selling "defective and mislabeled" merchandise.

The Verdict, Please . . .

The case melted under the scrutiny of Judge Edward Zaleski who dismissed it "with prejudice." He found the missing-peanut theory hard to swallow and concluded that the claim didn't amount to peanuts.

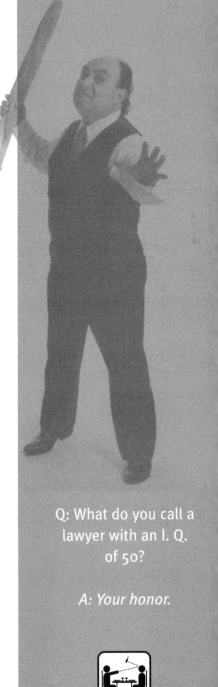

Q: What do you call a lawyer with an I. Q. of 50?

A: *Your honor.*

55

The Case of . . .

"THE UNCIVIL LIBERTARIAN"

Nicholas Vechione, Plaintiff, v. Sizzler Family Steakhouses, Defendant, in the Fourth District Court of Appeals of California

When Nicholas Vechione went to pay for his meal at a Sizzler restaurant, he was greeted with an unwelcome surprise. The cashier would not give him the $1.25 senior-citizen discount advertised prominently on the menu. The restaurant's reason? Nicholas Vechione was only thirty-one years old. This same civil rights crusader, who once sued Chippendale's to allow men to watch its strip shows, felt he was the victim of age discrimination. To satisfy his hunger for fairness, Vechione staked a claim against Sizzler in court.

The Verdict, Please . . .

The judge didn't think Vechione had much of a bone to pick and ruled in favor of the restaurant. For "making a mockery of the system," he was ordered to pay a fine of $8,601 (or about 850 *full-priced* meals). An appeals judge agreed that Vechione's beef was bogus.

Q: How many lawyers does it take to stop a moving bus?

A: *Never enough.*

56

The Case of . . .
"SIZZLIN' MAD"

William R. Lambeck, Plaintiff, v. George Salimes, Defendant, in the United States Court of Appeals for the Seventh Circuit

William Lambeck ordered his Sizzler steak cooked medium-well, but when the meal arrived, he turned red. The steak looked well-done, not medium-well. He demanded that he be brought a medium-well steak. According to the restaurant owner, the customer "was running up and down the dining room with his cellular phone and complaining to the waitress about the table, the salads, the meal, everything . . ."

Lambeck called the police from his cell phone "to get the situation corrected." When an officer arrived he told Lambeck to pay and get out, or face arrest. Expressing his distaste for the restaurant owner, the town's police department, and even the chief of police, Lambeck sued the bunch of them.

The Verdict, Please . . .

A district court judge skewered Lambeck's claim and tossed it out of court. He also ordered $16,000 in sanctions against him and his lawyer for filing a frivolous lawsuit. An appeals court judge agreed that Lambeck's argument was cooked up and he let stand the ruling that was originally served.

Q: Why are lawyers buried 25 feet underground?

A: 'Cause down deep they're real nice guys.

The Case of . . .

"THE TALE OF THE UNHAPPY MEAL"

Cory Brown, Plaintiff, v. McDonald's Corporation, Defendant, in the Atascadero Superior Court

When he bit into a pie at McDonalds, Cory Brown tasted more than apple filling—he tasted rodent. Brown had bit the head off of a whole mouse and, according to his attorney, fell to the ground and began vomiting and foaming at the mouth.

Brown sued McDonald's and their pie supplier, Bama Pie. There was only one problem: McDonald's investigators determined that Brown had planted the mouse, and that his suit was really a scheme to extort money from the burger empire. Among the evidence: 1) Pie filling is pumped through one-inch pipes, so the mouse could not have come through there; 2) Pies are cut into rectangles, yet the mouse was whole; 3) Pies are cooked at an internal temperature of 190° and enzyme tests conducted on the mouse determined that the rodent in Brown's pie never reached a temperature above 160°.

The Verdict, Please . . .

The judge smelled a rat here, especially since the mouse's tail was folded neatly along its body, indicating that someone had taken great care to insert the evidence. The judge refused to take the bait and ruled against Brown.

Q: You're trapped in a room with a lion, a tiger, and a lawyer. What do you do?

A: You shoot the lawyer, twice.

The Case of . . .
"A LEGAL APPETITE"

Vernon Tully, Plaintiff, v. McDonald's Corporation, Defendant, in the Supreme Court of Alabama

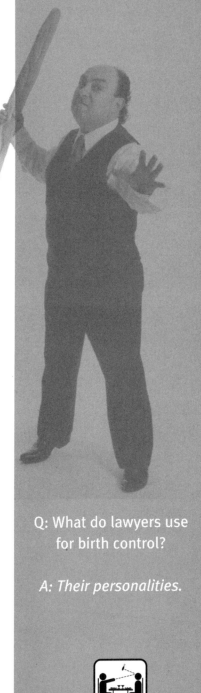

Vernon Tully loved to put on a good suit—a good *lawsuit*, that is. There was the time that he sued Coca-Cola because he allegedly found broken glass in the bottle—even though he claimed to have purchased the Coke while locked up in a prison that only served Pepsi. And then there was the time Tully sued *The Chattanooga Times* for running his obituary allegedly causing his wife and daughter tremendous emotional stress. Problem was, he didn't have a wife or daughter, and he had placed the notice himself. Tully also sued McDonald's, claiming to be a Muslim offended by the fast-food chain's reliance on "oils, greases, and lards containing animal by-products and pork." Citing race discrimination, he sued McDonald's again for not serving him hot sauce.

The Verdict, Please . . .

Vernon Tully's cases left a bad taste in the judges' mouths. For the false obituary, he was sentenced to sixty months' jail time and ordered to pay $20,000 in restitution to the *Times*. For the plaintiff's treating the judicial system like a food court, the judges spit out his suit against McDonald's.

Q: What do lawyers use for birth control?

A: *Their personalities.*

59

I'VE
FALLEN AND
I CAN'T
GET UP

The Case of . . .
"THE MOON SHOT"

Hank Reinfeld, Plaintiff, v. University of Idaho, Defendant, in the Idaho Bureau of Risk Management

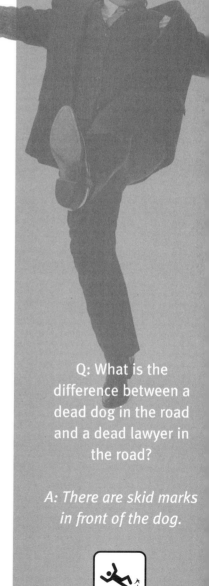

University of Idaho freshman Hank Reinfeld lived in a dorm with windows overlooking the street. Glancing down one afternoon, he noticed a couple of friends passing by. To get their attention he decided to "moon" them and climbed onto a heater, pulled down his pants, leaned his bare butt against the plate glass . . . and fell right through. Reinfeld plummeted three floors before landing on the ground, ultimately suffering a broken vertebra, compression fractures, deep cuts, and bruises on his hands, legs, and buttocks.

Wilkins left U of I and returned home to recuperate. While on the mend, the former freshman sued the university for not warning residents of the perilous nature of upper-story windows. Amused by the suit, residents of his dorm hung signs that read CAUTION!!! DO NOT PLACE BUTTOCKS AGAINST GLASS. PERSONAL INJURY MAY RESULT. Perhaps the greatest insult was delivered to Reinfeld via the *Lewiston Morning Tribune*, which ironically pointed out that Reinfeld "was not intoxicated" at the time of the incident. No doubt he wished he had been.

The Verdict, Please . . .

This was one small step for man, one giant leap for loony lawsuits. The lack of gravity of Reinfeld's argument caused the state to deny the claim—no ifs, ands, or butts.

Q: What is the difference between a dead dog in the road and a dead lawyer in the road?

A: *There are skid marks in front of the dog.*

61

The Case of . . .
"THE SHOCKING VERDICT"

Rose Smith, as Administratrix of the Estate of James Smith, Deceased, Plaintiff, v. New York City Transit Authority, Defendant,
in the Supreme Court of New York, Appellate Division, First Department

After a long day of squeegeeing car windshields, James Smith would often descend into the subway station at Broadway-Lafayette, which was filled with the city's downtrodden. One morning, in the station with his younger brother Earl, James slipped on a stray piece of garbage and fell onto the tracks. Thinking that a train was coming, James began running down the tracks, where he brushed up against the electrified third rail. Brother Earl jumped down after him, grabbed onto James, and was also walloped by the 600 volts of searing current.

The two brothers survived, but James suffered serious burns. The Smiths then sued New York City for negligence on the part of the Transit Authority. Their audacity stunned even hardened New Yorkers.

The Verdict, Please . . .

Despite the fact that Earl admitted to using cocaine that same morning and that the two were drinking just before the accident, a New York jury found in favor of the Smiths. They were awarded $13 million for pain, suffering, and loss of wages (which included approximately $9,000 for three years of James's lost wages as squeegee man). However, that amount was cut in half by the New York Supreme Court and a panel of appeals judges threw it out all together.

THE
WHIPLASH!
AWARD

Q: What is the difference between a lawyer and a hitman?

A: A hitman honors his contracts.

The Case of . . .
"STICKY FEET"

Heidi Flanders, Plaintiff, v. Furr's Supermarkets, Inc., Defendants, in the Court of Appeals of Texas, Eighth District, El Paso

Walking out of Furr's Supermarket in El Paso, Heidi Flanders suddenly tripped and fell. She then walked back inside the store and told the manager what had happened. The two then went outside to see what happened, and about six feet from where she stumbled, Flanders pointed to "something sticky between the size of a nickel and a quarter." Ms. Flanders concluded that the obstacle, a piece of old, dried chewing gum, was the culprit. She sued the grocery chain for "premises liability" due to her injuries and pain.

The Verdict, Please . . .

After chewing on it for a while, Judge Susan Larsen dismissed Flanders's claim, wondering aloud in court, "How does one trip on gum?"

Q: What do you call five thousand dead lawyers at the bottom of the ocean?

A: A good start!

63

DUMB
SUITS

The Case of . . .
"CLAP ON YOUR LAWSUIT!"

Gertrude Foley, Plaintiff, v. Joseph Enterprises, et al., Defendant, in the Supreme Court of New York, Appellate Division, Third Department

According to eighty year-old Gertrude Foley, her hands hurt so much that she couldn't even mash potatoes anymore. Her pain came from trying to work her "Clapper"—the gizmo advertised on television that remotely turns appliances on and off by clapping. Unlike on the commercials, Gertrude's clapping had no effect other than aggravating her arthritis. To compensate for her pain and suffering, she decided to get her mitts on the Clapper's creator in court.

The Verdict, Please . . .

It turned out that Foley was not too handy with gadgets. She had inadvertently set her Clapper's sensitivity control so low that a jackhammer wouldn't have set the thing off. The poor woman all but handed the court their decision against her. A Supreme Court judge agreed with the lower court's decision and dismissed the case hands down.

Q: What is the difference between a lawyer and a herd of buffalo?

A: *The lawyer charges more.*

The Case of . . .
"INATTENTION KMART CUSTOMERS!"

Betty Weist, Plaintiff, v. Kmart Corporation, Defendant

Betty Weist was browsing through a Kmart when she spotted a blender she wanted. But the blenders were stacked four high on an upper shelf and out of Weist's reach—well, almost. She jumped up and grabbed the bottom box in the stack. As she pulled, the three blenders above came crashing down and hit her on the head. Weist sued the retail giant, alleging "neck, shoulder, and back pain, and bilateral carpal-tunnel syndrome." Besides monetary damages, she took Kmart to task for "negligently stacking the boxes so high on the upper shelf."

The Verdict, Please . . .

Weist's admission that she knew the boxes would fall, blended with the fact that she didn't ask for help, did not mix well with the jury. It took them only a half hour to puree Weist's claims, and they found for "America's Store."

Q: How many lawyers does it take to change a lightbulb?

A : You won't find a lawyer who can change a lightbulb. Now, if you're looking for a lawyer to screw a lightbulb . . .

The Case of . . .
"NOT A LOTTO BRAINS"

Carolyn Counihan, Plaintiff, v. Pennsylvania Lottery Commission, Defendant, in the Westmoreland County Common Pleas Court

After years of playing and never winning the lottery, Carolyn Counihan realized that the odds of winning a lawsuit might be better than those of winning the lottery. She bet on beating the Pennsylvania Lottery Commission out of the $1.5 million that she, along with family and friends, had "invested" in their games. As Carolyn put it, "I have a legality issue here that I know you have a way to financially come through with what I am saying is already mine." With that kind of oratory as the backbone of her case, the odds of a victory seemed slim.

The Verdict, Please . . .

The plaintiff would have needed a lotto luck to have won this suit. In fact, she couldn't even find a lawyer to gamble on it. Counihan dropped the case and hopefully learned that making financial investments at the same place you can buy Cheese Curls and Slim Jims can be risky business.

Q: What do you call a lawyer gone bad?

A: Senator.

67

The Case of . . .
"CLIMB AND PUNISHMENT"

Ned P. Harris, Plaintiff, v. United States of America, Defendant,
in the United States District Court for the
Eastern District of California

The view from Moro Rock in Sequoia National Park turned out to be more electrifying than Ned Harris ever anticipated. Nearing the rock's peak, Harris was walloped by a lightning bolt from a storm that had just rolled in.

After recuperating from his injuries, Harris was still burning mad and took the 'National Park' Service to court. He claimed they "carelessly failed to provide any warning, guidance or supervision at all in respect of the danger of being struck by lightning." Apparently, Harris never heard about a certain scientist named Ben Franklin, nor his little experiment with a kite, a key, and a storm.

The Verdict, Please . . .

It was no shock that the judge felt this lawsuit was poorly grounded. He saw no power in the plaintiff's argument that the National Park Service was to blame for his current situation. The court pulled the plug on the case and ruled for the defendant.

Q: How can you tell when a lawyer is lying?

A: His lips are moving.

BAD
SPORTS

The Case of . . .

"THE OFFENSIVE TACKLE"

Shaniqua Jones, Plaintiff, v. Board of Education of Carroll County, Maryland, Defendant, in the Court of Special Appeals of Maryland

Shaniqua Jones was the first female high school football player in the history of Carroll County, Maryland. However, Shaniqua's career was short-lived. Running with the ball during her first scrimmage, she was tackled and suffered internal injuries.

Some two years later, Shaniqua sued the Board of Education of Carroll County for not warning her of the potential risk of injury in playing football. She admitted to knowing that football was a "physical contact sport," but based on what she'd seen on television she felt unlikely to receive much more than "a twisted ankle or something."

The Verdict, Please . . .

Shaniqua didn't score any points with the judge on her play for football damages. Concluding that she didn't have a legal cleat to stand on, the judge ruled against her. The plaintiff sought a replay before the court of appeals, but there too she gained no yardage.

The Case of . . .
"ATHLETE'S FOOT IN MOUTH"

Kenneth I. Kennedy, Plaintiff, v. Cypress Fairbanks Independent School District, Defendant, in the United States District Court

High school senior Kenneth Kennedy was furious about not getting a college athletic scholarship. He blamed his high school athletic director, Wayne Hooks, who replaced him as the football team's starting quarterback.

Ken took out his frustration in print by writing in his senior yearbook: "To Coach Hooks, I leave a $40,000 debt. I figure you cost me that much with your 3–7 season." Ken also used the memory book to question the masculinity of assistant baseball coach Brent McDonald. Not surprisingly, he was pulled from the pitching mound.

The athlete felt that he needed a supporter and took his claim to court. He sued the Cypress Fairbanks Independent School District for violating his constitutional right to take the pitching mound.

The Verdict, Please . . .

Unfortunately, Kenneth struck out in court. The umpire, in this case a federal judge, threw out his claim noting that "judges issue opinions and orders, not starting lineups." Perhaps the next time Ken tries to *write* a wrong he won't make the same error.

Q: What's the difference between a lawyer and a gigolo?

A: A gigolo only screws one person at a time.

71

The Case of . . .
"THE TEED-OFF GOLFER"

Elaine Newman, Plaintiff, v. Fort Kent Golf Club, Defendant,
in the Supreme Judicial Court of Maine

Golf for Elaine Newman became a real headache. On the first hole at the Fort Kent Golf Club, her shot landed near a set of railroad tracks that abutted the fairway. She swung away, but the ball ricocheted off the tracks and into her face. The bruised Newman sued the country club, despite the fact that golfers could see the tracks from the first tee, that Fort Kent management mapped out the tracks on the club's scorecard, and that they posted a warning sign at the tee.

The Verdict, Please . . .

Ironically, a trial court jury found Newman negligent for *not* using her head. However, they also drove to the conclusion that the country club shared some blame. The court swung a deal and awarded Newman $250,000, but lowered her winnings to $40,000, apparently handicapping her for ignoring all the warning signs.

Q: What do you do if you run over a lawyer?

A: Back over him to make sure. Then, make another notch on the steering wheel.

The Case of . . .

"THE ANGRY ATHLETIC SUPPORTER"

Harold L. Dillard, Plaintiff, v. Little League Baseball Incorporated, Defendant, in the Supreme Court of New York, Appellate Division, Fourth Department

Harold Dillard was filling in as a Little League umpire when nine-year-old pitcher John Rotondo tossed a wild pitch. Dillard called a time-out while the catcher retrieved the ball. But as the umpire turned his back to observe the catcher, the little pitcher threw the next pitch, striking Dillard in the groin. Dillard was angry at the peewee pitcher and struck back by suing Little League Baseball, Inc., for failing to provide him with a cup.

The Verdict, Please . . .

The judge felt that this case didn't deserve to get to second base. Noting the likelihood of "being struck by a baseball in the groin while umpiring," he tossed out the suit. An appeals court agreed that the judge's ruling was *safe.*

Q: What are lawyers good for?

A: *Making used-car salesmen look good.*

The Case of . . .

"THE MINOR-LEAGUE ATTITUDE"

Linda Lawrence, Plaintiff, v. Johnny Lupoli, Defendant, in the Appellate Court of Connecticut

Eight-year-old Little League pitcher Johnny Lupoli was warming up with practice throws when one of his pitches flew wildly toward the bleachers. His errant ball hit unsuspecting Linda Lawrence in the face and gave her quite a cut, which required sixty stitches to close.

The lacerated Lawrence decided to take the little shaver to court, claiming that she sustained permanent injuries including headaches, pains in her jaw, not to mention shock and anxiety. Stating that Johnny was careless, she sued him for negligence and loss of consortium (that she could no longer enjoy the pleasures of marital relations).

The Verdict, Please . . .

The judge dismissed the case and columnists cheered. However, little Johnny struck out on appeal. The appellate court reversed the dismissal and remanded the case to trial. It seems likely that the boy who *Chicago Tribune* writer Mike Royko dubbed Johnny "The Arm" will have his day in court.

Q: How do you get a lawyer out of a tree?

A: Cut the rope.

INJURED
FEELINGS

The Case of . . .

"GOOD-BYE, YELLOW BRICK ROAD"

Richard M. Klein, Plaintiff, v. City of San Diego, Defendant, in the United States District Court

After enduring a long line in the men's room during an Elton John–Billy Joel concert, Richard Klein approached the urinal expectantly. However, just as he unzipped his pants, a woman fed up with standing in an even longer line entered. Klein was unable to carry on with the task at hand and returned to his seat. Enduring duets of "River of Dreams" with a bulging bladder proved too much for Klein, and he sued the city for the embarrassment caused by "the presence of women in the restroom."

The Verdict, Please . . .

The judge felt his case was about as strong as a candle in the wind and blew it off. Adding insult to injury, the City of San Diego sought monetary sanctions against the plaintiff for filing a frivolous claim. All in all, a sad, sad song.

Q: How many lawyers does it take to change a lightbulb?

A: It only takes one lawyer to change your lightbulb to his lightbulb.

The Case of . . .

"A BIG BONE TO PICK"

Brenda Ballis, Plaintiff, v. New York State
Division of the Lottery, Defendant,
in the Supreme Court of New York

"Plus-sized" model Brenda Ballis was mortified. The five-foot-seven, two-hundred-pound woman saw a billboard urging New Yorkers to buy lottery tickets as an alternative to "marrying the client's big-boned daughter." The implication, that the only reason a man might marry a fat woman would be to kiss his boss's butt, caused her to take action. Speaking on behalf of "big-boned girls" everywhere, she took the New York State Division of the Lottery to court, seeking $1 million and an apology.

The Verdict, Please . . .

The claim didn't carry enough weight for the New York State Attorney General's office and they dropped it. But as luck would have it, media coverage of Ballis's lawsuit resulted in the airing of clips from her newly released exercise video. Coincidence? Fat chance!

Q: Why do lawyers never take their cats to the beach?

A: *Their cats keep trying to bury them with sand.*

The Case of . . .
"METHANE MADNESS"

Anthony R. Taper, Plaintiff, v. Randy Maresh, Defendant

Anthony Taper was disgusted by fellow checkout clerk Randy Maresh's flatulence problem. Taper claimed that the coworker disliked him and repeatedly farted in his direction. Fed up with Maresh's methane, Taper sued. His lawyer alleged that the "defendant has willfully and maliciously inflicted severe mental stress and humiliation on the plaintiff by conduct outrageous in the extreme by continually, intentionally, and repeatedly 'passing gas' directed toward the defendant." Taper's gas bill to Maresh came to $100,000.

The Verdict, Please . . .

Maresh's attorney thought the case against his client stunk and noted that Maresh's "expressive behavior" was protected by the First Amendment. The judge found the defendant's behavior "juvenile and boorish," but was unable to find any Oregon law prohibiting farting. He passed judgment that the case was legally full of hot air.

Q: What's the difference between a lawyer and a boxing referee?

A: A boxing referee doesn't get paid more for a longer fight.

EXPENSIVE
MEDICINE

The Case of . . .
"HARD TO STOMACH"

Arthur R. Bolger, Plaintiff, v. Humana Hospital Bayside, Defendant, in the Virginia Beach Circuit Court

Three-hundred-and-eight-pound Arthur Bolger knew that he had to do something about his weight and decided to have an operation in which doctors would staple his stomach to curb his appetite. The surgery was a success, and after implanting more than seventy tiny stainless-steel staples to constrict the patient's stomach, Dr. R. G. Brewer sent Bolger back to his hospital room to recuperate. But all that surgery must have made Arthur hungry, because he spotted a refrigerator down the hall and drank the milk he found inside. His binge caused the staples to burst, and he had to undergo emergency surgery.

After six weeks in intensive care, Bolger sued Humana Hospital for its insensitivity in leaving an unmonitored fridge within his vicinity. He sought a fat $250,000 for "enduring extreme pain and suffering and emotional distress."

The Verdict, Please . . .

The weight of evidence just wasn't there. Realizing the heavy burden of proof he needed to win his case, Bolger dropped the suit. Perhaps the gut buster should have had his jaw wired instead.

Q: Why is it that many lawyers have broken noses?

A: *From chasing parked ambulances.*

The Case of . . .
"AGGRAVATED ACNE"

Edward Wilden, Jr., Plaintiff, v. Frank E.Dunlap, M.D., et al., Defendants, in the Supreme Court of Illinois

Medical student Eddie Wilden suffered from a bad case of acne. His doctor, Dr. Frank Dunlap, prescribed the popular acne drug Accutane. Wilden had been on the medication for four months when one afternoon he went to a local forest preserve, spotted a fifteen-year-old boy, shoved him to the ground, and shocked the youngster with a stun gun. The next week, Wilden went back into the preserve and shocked a twenty-five-year-old man and grabbed the man's genitals while he kissed him.

Upon his arrest, Wilden pleaded guilty to misdemeanor battery. However, the governor of Illinois stepped in and pardoned the med student. Apparently, Wilden's clean prior record and letters on his behalf from Dr. Dunlap influenced the call from the governor. But the case then took on an even stranger complexion when the newly pardoned Wilden sued Dr. Dunlap, claiming he had failed to adequately monitor his condition, which caused him to assault his two victims.

The Verdict, Please . . .

A case of Clearasil couldn't clear up the logic of this case. The judge found in favor of Dr. Dunlap and dismissed all of Wilden's charges, but an appellate court overturned the judgment and prescribed that the case go to trial.

Q: What is the difference between a lawyer and a trampoline?

A: You take off your shoes to jump on a trampoline!

The Case of . . .

"NOT IN THE CARDS"

Sarina Evans, Plaintiff, v. Temple University Hospital, Defendant, in the Philadelphia Court of Common Pleas

Psychic Sarina Evans used to be able to read people's auras. However, after a scan at Philadelphia's Temple University Hospital, Evans's attempts at marshaling her powers of perception left her with only a headache. She claimed that the X ray destroyed her psychic business and sued the hospital for malpractice. An adverse reaction to the dye injected prior to the CAT scan caused Evans to go into "anaphylactic shock," according to her attorney.

Evans convinced police officers to testify on her behalf, supporting her claim that she had used her psychic powers to help them solve cases. However, while Evans's clairvoyance was strong enough to collar criminals, it didn't warn her away from Temple University Hospital.

The Verdict, Please . . .

The future looked bright for the plaintiff when a jury awarded her $986,465. However, happiness for Evans was not in the stars. After calling the damages "grossly excessive as to shock the court's sense of justice," Judge Leon Katz threw out the verdict . . . But maybe Evans knew that all along.

BIZARRE
CASES

The Case of . . .

"THE CREEPY CRAWLER"

Barbara Delone, Plaintiff, v. National Corporation for Housing Partnerships, Defendant, in the Richmond Circuit Court

Barbara Delone was napping in her comfortable recliner when she suddenly woke up with a "sharp pain" in her ear. She got up, and with each step the pain increased. Delone ran outside for help, where a neighbor found her clutching a light pole screaming in agony.

It turns out that while Delone slept, a cockroach climbed into her ear and began chewing a hole in her eardrum. Members of the local rescue squad flushed the roach from her ear. Though Delone's doctor assured her that ear tissue regenerates, she nevertheless sued her building for negligence.

The Verdict, Please . . .

Delone could not get the bug out of her head that she was owed something for the encroachment she suffered. To avoid a trial, her building reached a settlement. Interestingly, her doctor noted that "there is a problem with roaches more than other bugs because I understand roaches can't walk in reverse."

The Case of . . .
"SO WHO YOU GONNA CALL?"

Alan Sosney, Plaintiff, v. Helen V. Ackley, Defendant, in the Supreme Court of New York, Appellate Division, First Department

Helen Ackley owned a haunted house and was proud of it. In an interview with *Reader's Digest* she insisted that her large Victorian house was possessed by poltergeists. When Ackley eventually put her house up for sale, she had no problem scaring up a buyer. Alan Sosney happily paid the $650,000 asking price, until, that is, he realized he might have to spend the rest of his life listening to chains rattle in the attic.

Upon learning about the house's additional inhabitants, Sosney sued Ackley for neglecting to inform him that the house was haunted. This case was definitely one for the *Trialite Zone.*

The Verdict, Please . . .

This case didn't have a ghost of a chance, according to a lower court judge, but an appellate judge disagreed and sent it to trial. He noted that Ackley violated the law, since the existence of ghosts meant that she had not left her house vacant. The appellate judge feared the idea of "a psychic or medium routinely accompanying the structural engineer and Terminex man on an inspection of every home."

Q: Why won't vultures eat dead lawyers?

A: There are some things that would gag even a vulture.

85

The Case of . . .
"A BAD BREAK"

Bradley E. Frankel, Plaintiff, v. Victoria Lee Howell, Defendant, in the Floyd County Small Claims Court

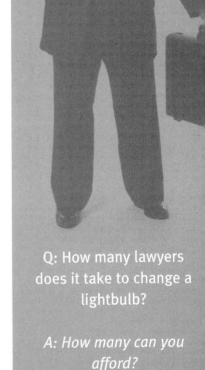

"Breaking up is hard to do," as the song goes. But Victoria Lee Howell would never have guessed that dumping her boyfriend would land her in court. However, that's just what happened when Brad Frankel sued her, alleging that as part of their breakup, the two had a "sex for money" deal at $100 per session.

The plaintiff claimed that he paid Howell a total of $1,800, but that they had intercourse only three times. Stating that "she owes me fifteen sessions or $1,500," Brad sought a branch of the judicial system for a snap judgment.

The Verdict, Please . . .

The details on what finally happened after this rocky romance ended are sketchy. However, if the plaintiff's claims were true, one must admire the entrepreneurial spirit in selling "breakup packages."

Q: How many lawyers does it take to change a lightbulb?

A: How many can you afford?

87

The Case of . . .

"ATTORNEY, CLIENT PRIVILEGE"

Rachel Ryder, Plaintiff, v. Paul A. Golden, Defendant, in the Supreme Court of New York, New York County

Rachel Ryder appreciated the way attorney Paul Golden guided her through her difficult divorce proceedings, after which the two went on with their lives. Two years later, Ryder and Golden ran into each other. It did not take long for their prior professional relationship to blossom into a love affair. Ryder soon sold her apartment, moved into Golden's, and they jointly bought a vacation house.

Unfortunately, the relationship did not last, and over the next several years Ryder reflected on why Golden broke up with her. Ryder concluded that she was a victim unable to resist Golden's sexual advances due to a "transference response" to this authoritative figure who was once her attorney. She sued her ex-esquire, claiming rape, battery, and fraud.

The Verdict, Please . . .

This case gives new meaning to the phrase "power of attorney." Nevertheless, the judge thought the plaintiff's argument was weak. Blaming your attorney for being too charming is apparently a tough case to sell. In this suit of lover v. lawyer, the law won.

Q: Where can you find a good lawyer?

A: In the cemetery!

The Case of . . .
"MIAMI ADVICE"

Susan Dennis, Plaintiff, v. William R. Dennis, Defendant, in the Supreme Court of Washington

Tourists Susan and William Dennis had not chosen the best of spots in Miami to spend their money. They realized this when a store employee advised them "to hurry up and get to the car because it gets quite dangerous when the police leave." On their way out of the parking lot, William asked the parking attendant for directions. He advised William to turn left out of the lot, but he decided to go right instead, telling Susan that they would "take the scenic route." They soon became lost and Bill advised his wife to "shut [her] mouth" every time she made a suggestion.

Bill finally agreed to pull over and examine his map, when a rock smashed through the window and a hand reached into the car. He sped away and soon realized that Susan had been injured by the shattered glass. After arriving back home in Washington, Susan decided to sue her husband for negligence in not adequately ensuring her safety.

The Verdict, Please . . .

Ms. Dennis should have mapped out a better legal strategy. She was obviously unaware that the failure to ask for directions is a matter of male genetics, not negligence. Her argument went the wrong way and the court found in favor of her first mate. While Mr. Dennis may have been pleased, his marriage was clearly headed for a bad course.

Q: How many lawyers does it take to change a lightbulb?

A: Three. One to change it and two to keep interrupting by standing up and shouting "Objection!"

SMALL CLAIMS

The Case of . . .
"TORTS FOR TOTS"

Nina Davis, Plaintiff, v. Jonathan Bianchi, Defendant, in the Suffolk Superior Court

Three-year-old Nina Davis was playing in the sandbox when another three year old, Jonathan Bianchi, ran up and kicked her. Nina's mother, Anne, scolded him sternly. Not one to allow her son to be taken to task by another mother, Jonathan's mother, Margareth, yelled back at Anne Davis.

Resenting the proverbial sand being kicked in her face, Davis fired back with a lawsuit. She sought a restraining order against Margarth *and* her son that would cover "all times and all places."

The Verdict, Please . . .

As petty as this argument sounded, the judge actually granted Davis a restraining order over the sandbox skirmish. The local media accused both judge and the plaintiff of small-mindedness and the Fort Lauderdale *Sun-Sentinel* expressed the hope that for the child's sake, "a lack of common sense is not hereditary."

Q: Why are lawyers good lovers?

A: They have a lot of experience screwing.

91

The Case of . . .
"THE TRAGIC KINGDOM"

Norma Lambeck, Plaintiff, v. The Walt Disney Company, Defendant, in the Orange County Superior Court

Former Mouseketeer Norma Lambeck wanted to share the wonders of Disneyland with her grandchildren and off they went to the famous amusement park. They had a great day on the rides, but unfortunately, their pleasure was short-lived. Walking back to their car in the parking lot, they were held up at gunpoint and she lost $1,650 in cash and jewelry.

The robbery was just the beginning of Lambeck's emotional trauma. She and her family returned to the park to report the theft, where they were taken "backstage." There the tykes saw various Disney characters removing the heads from their costumes and were shocked that the characters . . . weren't real! Outraged by her grandchildren's premature loss of innocence, Lambeck took Disney to court, alleging negligence and infliction of severe emotional distress.

The Verdict, Please . . .

For the Lambecks, Disneyland was anything but "The Happiest Place on Earth." Disney asserted in their court papers that "there's no duty on the part of Disneyland to hide the truth." The judge apparently agreed and thought the legal grounds were Mickey Mouse. The court ruled for the Magic Kingdom.

Q: Why do scientists prefer lawyers to rats for their experiments?

A: Lawyers are more plentiful than rats.

92

The Case of . . .
"THE CRACKER JACK LAWYER"

Deborah Winkler, Plaintiff, v. Borden, Inc., Defendant, in the Hamilton County Court

As soon as nine-year-old Debbie Winkler ripped into her unopened box of Cracker Jacks, she dug toward the bottom for the toy surprise. Finding none, Winkler's excitement turned to disappointment. The little girl, her mother recalls, "was so sad-faced." Wendy's father, Saul, could not stand the thought that his little girl might have to live with her heartbreak, and he helped her write a letter to Borden, the manufacturer.

When, after two weeks the Winklers received no reply, Saul decided to teach his daughter that every mistake has its price: Winkler sued the snack maker, and sought damages in the amount of one complimentary box of Cracker Jacks and reimbursement for court costs. Frustrated upon finding the box empty of its promised toy surprise, the world-weary nine year old said, "I feel since I bought their product because of their claim, they broke a contract with me."

The Verdict, Please . . .

Young Winkler dropped her suit when she received an apology and a coupon for a complimentary box of Cracker Jacks. The company did not, however, include a check for her $19 court costs. According to a Borden spokesperson, "We had sent the coupon and note of apology to Wendy about thirteen working days after we got a letter of complaint from her, but before she got our letter, the suit was filed." Mr. Winkler was convinced, however, that his disgruntled daughter learned an invaluable lesson: "I told her, whenever you can settle out of court, it's just as important as suing somebody."

Q: Did you hear about the terrorist that hijacked a 747 full of lawyers?

A: He threatened to release one every hour if his demands weren't met.

93

TONY BUTTAFONY'S
INSIDER'S GUIDE TO
LAWYERSPEAK

What They Say	*What They Mean*
Accessory to a crime	Business partner
Attorney-client privilege	Honor among thieves
Billable hours	Your piece of my three-hundred-hour workweek
Case of malpractice	Case of Dom Pérignon
Class-action suit	Gang bang
Contingency fee	New Lexus for me
Retainer fee	New Lexus for my secretary
Expert witness	Rent-a-witness
Irrelevant and immaterial	I didn't think of that
Protracted litigation	Annuity
Legally true	Probably false
Members of the jury	My twelve new best friends
May it please the court	May I kiss your ass
My client has no recollection	My client remembers all too well
My client was abused as a child	My client abused a child
My client pleads insanity	My client is screwed
My client pleads the Fifth	My client is so guilty I could down a fifth
Temporary insanity	Sometimes you feel like a nut . . .

ABOUT THE AUTHOR AND CONTRIBUTORS

Author: James Percelay is a comedy writer and producer who created the best-selling *SNAPS* book series and television shows. His background includes producing the parody commercials on *Saturday Night Live* and documentaries ranging from *The Dance Theater of Harlem* to *The Rolling Stones*. James was head of development at Hearst Entertainment and has produced projects for all the major networks. He developed a series for USA network and is currently developing *THUNK*, television's first real-time animated game show, as well as new humor books.

Contributing Editor: Jeremy Deutchman is a Harvard University graduate student by day and a writer by night. He is a Phi Beta Kappa graduate of the University of California at Berkeley, with a double major in religion and Spanish. Jeremy has been published in *Tikkun* magazine and in Harvard's *Mosaic* journal.

"Tony Buttafony, Esq.": Sal Petraccione is a New York–based actor/comedian who has been featured on television series including *Friends, Law & Order, The Sopranos,* and *New York Undercover,* as well as in films, theater, and commercials.

Cover photo:	Adam Weiss
Interior photos:	Kristine Larsen
Logo designer:	Dylan Haley
Photo effects artist:	Vi Nguyen

ACKNOWLEDGMENTS

The AUTHOR hereby thanks the following parties, heretofore referred to as FRIENDS, for their assistance, support, and/or encouragement:

Fred Graham, Judge Mills Lane, Lionel, Bill Maher, Dennis Miller, Craig Kilborn, Phil "Jackie Chiles" Morris, Bill O'Reilly, Geraldo Rivera, Dan Quayle, Howard Stern, John Stossel.

ICI Dyepack, M&M/Mars, New York Transit Authority, Ogden Entertainment.

Dr. John Abroon, Vincent and Donna Anelle, Mercedes Ayala, Naomi Boak, Mike Cioara, Laura Brown, Phil Campanella, Goodies, Juan Pablo Cappello, Esq., Cloudy Brothers (Skipper Davis, Keith Heard, Little Tiny Heard, Homer Jolly, Jimmy Kennedy, Doug Curtiss), "New York Joe" Catalfumo, George Ciccarone, Chris Cohen, Bernard D'Orazio, Esq., Pat DeRosa, Bruce Feinberg, Trisha Ferrone, John Franklin III, Gerald Frazier of the NYC Transit Authority, Phil Galinsky, Renee Glicker, Dr. Steven Glickman, Goodies, Sheila Griffiths, Anthony Grasso, Phil Graves, Barry and Betty Lou Kibrick, Dr. Allen Kozin, Linus Lee, David J. Leiter, Phil Lebovits, Jeffrey Lutsky, Lou Martini, Alan Potashnick, Jim and Inez McGee, Brother Frank Minucci, Bobby Miranda, Arthur Nascarella, Portabella Pizza, Andy Nulman, Scott Papacuri, Lew Perlman, Mario Occhicone, Victor Pabone, Paul Ruffo, Esq., Tony Ray Rossi, Jon Sanpietro, James Signorelli, Peggy Smith, Alan and Anita Sosne, Eric Solstein, Dr. Gary Takowski,

Andrew Vanderhauten, Dr. Fran Vogler, Nick Wickersham, Tony Winchester, Paul and G.G. Weisenfeld, Frank Wolf.

Court TV
Henry Schleiff, President

Michigan Lawsuit Abuse Watch (M-LAW)
Robert B. Dorigo Jones, President

Citizens Against Lawsuit Abuse (CALA)
Anthony Bell, Executive Director

American Tort Reform Association (ATRA)
Sherman Joyce, President

Pennsylvania Attorney General Mike Fisher

"Some men are heterosexual, and some are bisexual, and some don't think about sex at all—they become lawyers."

—Woody Allen

"Lawyers today are like gamblers . . . they take on lawsuit, after lawsuit, after lawsuit until eventually they find a jury wacky enough to award money."

—Howard Stern

"Lawyers: persons who write a ten-thousand-word document and call it a brief."

—Franz Kafka

"Lawsuits are seeds planted by lawyers."

—Dennis Miller

"The first thing we do, let's kill all the lawyers."

—Shakespeare, *King Henry VI*